Taste.

When we trave[l,] encounters and visual impress[ions.] It is the sensual experiences th[at shape] our memories. It's the smells a[nd tastes that make] every place in the world uniqu[e.]

We've visited over 30 cities to experience them as closely as possible for our travel guides. We got to know many interesting personalities, including chefs and restaurant operators. Every meal shaped our feeling for each city. It is these culinary inspirations that we want to share with you. To bring the special creations of our favourite chefs to your private dining table.

Our curiosity on our travels is as limitless as the recipe ideas in this book are diverse. However, we never want to forget about the possibility of implementation, and with this premise we have asked our friends at the stove around the world to support us with their ideas.

The result is a wild ride through legendary kitchens. A Brooklyn neighbourhood institution shares an American bar snack from the 1950s. A Berlin minimalist with a Michelin star takes purism to the extreme and cooks a turnip. The signature dish of a London cult restaurant is not for the faint of heart.

Get lost in a world of flavours.

3
Editorial

Stories

28
Meeting Coney
Margot Guicheteau

40
Living Food
Jieun Choi

Recipes

6
Olmsted, NYC
Crab Rangoons

10
Tawlet, Beirut
Tabbouleh

14
Dishoom, London
Kejriwal

22
Nobelhart & Schmutzig, Berlin
Celeriac

54
Bar del Pla, Barcelona
Pig's Trotters

32
Matur og Drykkur, Reykjavik
Salted Cod

36
Cavalariça, Comporta
Sea Bream

42
Tabaré, NYC
Potato & Beet Gnocchi

46
St. John, London
Pot Roast

58
St. Bart, Berlin
Rosewater Pavlova

62
Ingredients

63
Playlists

Greg Baxtrom, Olmsted, New York City

The Agriculturalist

A former fine-dining chef is getting back to basics

Resourceful Finesse

After working at fine-dining institutions such as Alinea, Per Se, Atera, and Blue Hill at Stone Barns, Greg Baxtrom opened his own restaurant and took it down a notch. Olmsted may be a laid-back Brooklyn neighbourhood restaurant, but the menu is serious, with ingredients chosen out of a deep respect for nature's bounty and the art of agriculture. Having grown up in a farmhouse with a lot of time spent in nature as a scout, Baxtrom later rediscovered the importance of sustainable and local sourcing while working at Blue Hill. Growing produce with good soil, often in the restaurant's own backyard garden, became an essential part of Olmsted's identity, and the reason why the chef's seasonal menus have garnered a loyal following.

Greg, what is the personal story behind this dish?
Crab Rangoons is a dish my sister always ordered separately from what we were ordering as a group when we were younger. I was thinking of her when I put together this recipe. When designing the Olmstead menu I realised we hadn't used any crab yet, and there was this great purveyor at the time also selling to Blue Hill and other restaurants. So I decided to marry the two ideas into this dish. And of course, we had to serve it with the neon red sauce that always comes with rangoons.

Why did you decide to open a laid-back local restaurant after working at fine-dining venues?
A mentor of mine once told me that when I was ready to open my own place, I needed to be comfortable being in my own restaurant. When it was time to open Olmsted, I realised I didn't really want to eat three- or six-hour meals anymore. I wanted to open a restaurant where not only I was comfortable, but where my mom would be comfortable eating too.

Any tips for home cooks who want to make simpler meals more in tune with nature?
I would start by going to the produce section and looking for things that weren't there the week before. It's a good indication that something is in season, and can be a good gateway into tasting more fresh local produce that tends to require less work in the kitchen.

Crab Rangoons

The dish with Burmese roots first appeared under that name in 1956 on the menu of Tiki-style restaurant Trader Vic's in San Francisco.

Ingredients

Makes 10–12 pieces
450 g (1 cup) picked crab meat
250 g (1 cup) fresh ricotta cheese
225 g (1 cup) sautéed & chopped kale, let it cool
1 pack store-bought wonton wrappers
Oil for frying
1000 ml (4 ¼ cups) orange juice
1000 ml (4 cups) glucose syrup
500 ml (2 cups) red wine vinegar
200 g (2 cups) sugar
1 bulb of garlic
1 Fresno pepper, halved
20 g (1/8 cup) Szechuan pepper
1 bunch cilantro chopped
96 g (3 tbsp) Calabrian Chilli
Salt to taste
Lemon juice to taste
White soy—Shiro is a light Japanese soy sauce, to taste
Download ingredient lists p. 62

Preparation

Sweet & Sour Chilli Sauce
1. Combine and bring to boil the orange juice, glucose, vinegar, sugar, garlic, cilantro, and Fresno pepper in a saucepan over a medium heat.
2. Simmer to desired consistency. Finish with the lemon juice, white soy sauce and salt, and check the flavour. Remove from heat, add the Szechuan pepper and let it cool.

Crab Rangoons
1. In a mixing bowl add the crab meat, ricotta cheese, and chopped kale while the ingredients are still cold and mix well. Divide the filling into 10–12 wonton wrappers. To make a triangle Crab Rangoon, fold up the wonton wrap to form a triangle. Pinch the edges to seal tight.
2. In a deep-frying pan or a pot heat the oil until it reaches 175°C (350°F). Fry the wontons for 3 minutes. Drain excess oil with paper towels.
3. Serve with sweet and sour chilli sauce.

Setting

Matching Mood
To keep your cocktail-driven late Friday afternoon in a crunchy balance.

Matching Drink
A Royal Hawaiian Mai Tai.

Matching Music
A 1950–60s Tiki-inspired soundtrack, featuring legends like Yma Sumac, Dick Dale and Lee Baxter.
Listen to matching playlists p. 63

Kamal Mouzawak, Tawlet, Beirut

Levantine Dreams

A restaurateur's quest to connect his country through food

Beirut

Building Bridges

One encounters certain concepts through life and wonders, "How come no one thought of that before?"

Kamal Mouzawak created such a concept. Once a week a chef from a different region in Lebanon comes to his restaurant and works the ovens. That means guests can travel through diverse regional cuisines with limited movement. This was subliminal inspiration for the book currently in your hand. Lebanon, a country with much history and many influences, has a lot to dig into. For better or worse its complexity is a source of beauty. This recipe, through its simplicity but difficulty in perfecting, makes the ideal window into this country.

What is so special about the dish you present here?

Tabbouleh is Lebanon's national dish ... it is as colourful, fresh and mixed as Lebanon is—there is no Sunday meal or festive lunch without a tabouleh—and abroad, only fake and weird versions are known ... Better to spread the real one!

Lebanon is a such small country but you have a huge local variety in the cooking. What are the main styles and differences?

First of all there are two different cuisines —the public, which takes the form or street or souk food, or mezze in the restaurant. Then, there is the private; regional, seasonal home cooking that's totally different from restaurant food. Home cooking is very diverse as it is regional. As small as Lebanon is, it has a very diverse geography, with coastal plain, high mountains, and continental lands of the Bekaa Valley—and origins of people—making the cuisine very diverse.

What dish (apart from the one here) represents the taste of Lebanon perfectly? And where to try it in Beirut?

There's not one—but one for each region. A kebbeh arnabyieh with all kinds of citrus as a taste of the coastal plain, eaten at Tawlet Saida; a manousheh as a taste of the high mountains eaten at any street side saj; and keshek as a taste of the Bekaa Valley, eaten at Tawlet Ammiq.

What major spices define Lebanese cuisine?

Spices are more of a city product, and cities are coastal—and open to trade, exchange, wealth and foreign products. We use a kind or pepper we call sweet pepper or Lebanese 7 spices—like the American all-spice.

What's the most interesting meal you've had in the last ten years (and where)?

In Lebanon, a lunch at Georgina in Kfar Dlekos in the north. Abroad, a lunch at Da Gemma in Rodinno in Piedmont, Italy.

Tabbouleh

»Variations and interpretations are of course possible, but for the love of tabbouleh … call them something else.«—Kamal Mouzawak

Ingredients

Serves 4
2 bunches (about 150 g / 2 ½ cups each) of flat leaf parsley, washed and dried, finely chopped
A small bunch (about 75 g / 1 ¼ cup) of mint, washed and dried, strip the leave
2 medium spring onions, trimmed, thinly sliced
1 large ripe tomato, chopped into small dices
115 g (1/2 cup) fine bulgur—for a non-crunchy bulgur version, wash the bulgur, drain, and keep it covered in a little water to soak.
Juice of 2 lemons
1/3 cup (about 73 g) olive oil
Salt and pepper
Green hot pepper, finely diced (optional)
Romaine lettuce or tender white cabbage leaves to serve

Preparation

1. In a mixing bowl add tomato and bulgur and parsley. Finely chop mint leaves then add to the bowl.
2. Rub sliced spring onions with salt and pepper, then add to with the rest of the ingredients.
3. Dress the tabbouleh with lemon juice, olive oil and salt, as needed. The tabbouleh should be juicy, without swimming in liquid. It is a fresh, slightly acidic salad.

Setting

Matching Mood
Bringing the whole family together for a Sunday lunch in the garden.

Matching Drink
Arak mixed with water and ice.

Matching Music
Timeless tabbouleh fits with classics from Fairuz to contemporary Elias Rahbani.

Daniela Prasuna Coppini, La Paloma, Ibiza

Family Ties

An Italian chef shares her grandson's favourite dish

Secret Garden

In the small village of San Lorenzo, right in the middle of Ibiza, chef Daniela Prasuna Coppini and her family have created a little culinary world for themselves consisting of dream produce and time-crafted recipes from Italy. What was once a run-down finca is now a restaurant among the citrus orchards built with the help of locals and a touch of magic.

Having learned to cook from her mother in Tuscany, and refined her style through her travels, Daniela creatively fuses Italian recipes with the spices and flavours of other cuisines. The small menu is always different, but what doesn't change are the ingredients; sourced locally, imported directly from Italy, or grown in the restaurant's own little garden.

Daniela, why did you choose to share this dish?
My grandson chose this dish. He likes ceviche very much, and that for me personally is the interesting story behind it... Also because it's an easy recipe to make at home.

Which ingredients do you prefer to import from Italy?
I use capers from Pantelleria in Sicily, and the Parmesan cheese—which is one of the best—comes from a wonderful family with a farm near Reggio Emilia with whom I've been working since the beginning of La Paloma. The salami, ham, and cheese that are part of the Antipasto Toscano, I get from Pollen, a beautiful shop here on the island run by a young and beautiful family who get their products directly from Tuscany.

What advice would you give home cooks to eat simpler and more consciously?
My advice is to always eat veggies that are in season and to research markets that sell local products. When it's not possible to buy local, always choose good quality, and avoid canned foods and industrial products. I personally prefer to eat simpler but with attention to the quality. I always look at the ingredients, preferring organic without preservatives.

You grew up in Tuscany but like to fuse Italian recipes with other cuisines. How has living in Ibiza changed the way you cook?
I lived in India for a while and that's where my love for spices began. I have always been a lover of good food, no matter from where, because I also love to combine flavours from all over the world when cooking. Being here in Ibiza gave me the inspiration to keep going with this passion of fusion food.

Ibiza

Salmon Ceviche

Ceviche is a seafood dish originally from Peru. Today all over Latin America a wide variety of interpretations can be found, differing in ingredients and preparation.

Ingredients

Serves 6

600 g (ca 1.30 lb) of quality salmon fillet (preferably wild, otherwise organically farmed), skin removed
Juice of 2 limes
Juice of 1 lemon
Juice of ½ orange
150 g (1 cup) celery finely sliced
3 spring onions, finely sliced
1 chilli pepper (preferably jalapeño)
1 ripe mango, diced
1 bunch of coriander, chopped
Good quality extra virgin olive oil
Salt to taste

Preparation

1. Clean and pat dry the salmon fillet and cut into about ½ inch (over 1 cm) pieces.
2. In a glass or stainless steel bowl, combine the citrus juice and salmon. Let the salmon marinate for 30 minutes.
3. Drain the liquid. Add the rest of the ingredients except salt and olive oil and mix well. Season with salt, dress with the olive oil and serve.

Setting

Matching Mood
When summer nights get exciting and there is no time to cook.

Matching Drink
A white wine from Campania in Italy, like the full-bodied Donnachiara Greco di Tufo.

Matching Music
Some smooth Balearic tunes compiled by veteran Ibizan DJs with Italian roots like Leo Mas or DJ Pippi.

Naved Nasir, Dishoom, London

Bombay Beat

London's Indian food empire shares a breakfast classic

Magical Journey

Navid Nasir was a chef in Bombay for almost a decade before moving to London and joining the Dishoom team in 2010. His love for the megapolis is evident in his dishes, and working alongside culinary fanatics from Southeast Asia (who have also spent time in Bombay) adds to the authentic feeling that's made Dishoom a staple on the London food scene. Apart from the original location, meanwhile, there are four more branches in London and three in other UK cities—all different but aesthetically designed, with a nostalgic nod.

Regular research trips to Bombay, when the team indulges in vada pau fresh from the street-side fryer, or glasses of chai from the city's much-loved Irani cafés, also help in this endeavour. As does an obsession with every detail, whether it's the design of the crockery or the flavour of the dishes carried on them. Nashir's version of Kejriwal transforms a popular Indian afternoon snack into a spicy start to the day.

Kejriwal

»*Chilli-cheese toast is a real favourite of Bombayites, and a regular fixture on our table whenever we visit the much-loved Leopold Cafe in Bombay. Kejriwal takes this afternoon snack and transforms it into a first-rate breakfast with the addition of perfectly fried eggs.*«—Naved Nasir

Ingredients

Serves 3–4
160 g (2 cups) mature cheddar, grated
2–4 thick slices of white bread, sourdough, or brioche (depending on size and level of hunger)
4 spring onions, chopped
2 green chillies, very finely chopped
2 tsp vegetable oil (optional)
2 to 4 large eggs (one per slice of toast)
Coarsely ground black pepper
Tomato ketchup to serve

Preparation

1. Let the grated cheese come to at room temperature; it needs to be quite soft and workable. Preheat the oven to 240°C (475°F)/Fan 220°C (425°F)/Gas 9. Place a baking tray inside to warm up.
2. In a toaster toast the bread until very lightly browned on both sides. Set

LONDON

aside to cool slightly while you prepare the topping. Put aside a small handful of the grated cheese (20 g or 1/4 cup), 2 tsp chopped spring onion, and a pinch of green chilli, to be used when you fry the eggs. Crack the eggs into a cup or small bowl, being careful to keep the yolks intact.

3. Put the remaining cheese, spring onions and green chilli into a bowl, add plenty of black pepper and mix well. By using the back of a spoon (or your fingers), work the cheese mixture into a paste by pressing it firmly into the side of the bowl.

4. Spread the cheese mix evenly over the toast and press it in, using the back of the spoon, to create a firm, even layer that goes all the way to the edges of the toast. Place on the tray in the oven and bake for 6–8 minutes, until a deep golden colour and bubbling. While the chilli cheese toast is cooking, warm a frying pan over high heat and add the oil. Gently tip the eggs into the hot pan and add some black pepper. Top with the reserved grated cheese, spring onion and green chilli. Place the frying pan in the oven and bake for 2 minutes, or until the cheese is melted and the egg whites are cooked but the yolks are still runny.

5. Place two cheese toasts on a plate, carefully slide the eggs (gently separate the egg—one egg per toast) onto the melted cheese on toast and serve immediately, with plenty of tomato ketchup.

| Setting |

Matching Mood
With a good morning read—perhaps the local news in India's oldest English-language newspaper, The Indian Times.

Matching Drink
A glass of sweet chai.

Matching Music
Indian classical music from performers such as Shivkumar Sharma, Hari Prasad Chaurasia, Zakir Hussain, or Ravi Shankar.

Legend has it that Kejriwal is named after a Bombayite who used to ask for the dish because his wife forbade him to eat eggs at home.

Micha Schäfer, Nobelhart & Schmutzig, Berlin

Into the Green

Excellent produce is the key to minimalist cuisine

Enchanted Forest

The recipe book of German fine dining was torn up by notorious sommelier Billy Wagner. Together with chef Micha Schäfer he is the mastermind behind the concept of the restaurant Nobelhart und Schmutzig.

They opened it in 2015; close to the old border that formerly sliced Berlin into two countries. And east and west matters not when it comes to ingredients—every component comes from the city and its surrounding countryside. The team works directly with farmers and producers to source the goods.

These strictly local flavours permeate the ten-course set menu, which is a feast of craft and purity. Diners enjoy it at the u-shaped bar, accompanied by the exquisite sounds of vinyl records from the owner's collection.

The dish presented here conveys Schäfer's minimalistic approach, reflecting the importance of sustainable agriculture. It might have been conceived in a Michelin Star kitchen, but you can now emulate the chef's genius in your own kitchen for some selected lucky ones.

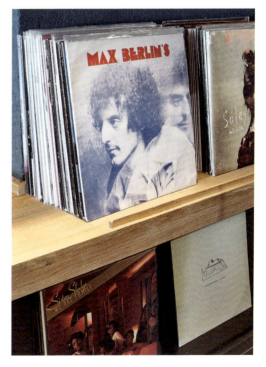

Celeriac and Blackcurrant Wood Oil

»For everything we cook it is very important to source the produce very carefully. If you don't have an amazing carrot or strawberry, the dish will not only be pointless but also pretty awful. Also, whenever you have an amazing product in your hands and you're wondering how you could make this into something even better, that's the way to go.«—Micha Schäfer

Ingredients

Serves 2
1 celeriac
50 g (a little less than a ¼ cup) double cream
1 l (4 ¼ cup) rapeseed oil
A handful of freshly chopped blackcurrant wood
Salt

Preparation

1. To make the blackcurrant wood oil, place the blackcurrant wood in a pot, cover with rapeseed oil, and leave to cook overnight at 70°C (160°F). Strain it. (As an alternative to the blackcurrant wood oil, use best quality hazelnut, walnut, linseed dottera or olive oil).
2. Scrub the celeriac until clean and rub well with rapeseed oil and salt. Preheat oven at 180°C (350°F). Cook in the oven whole for 1 hour and then finish at 210°C (450°F) for a further 15 minutes. Once the celeriac is cooked, remove it from the oven.
3. Cut the celeriac into eight pieces. Drizzle them with the blackcurrant wood oil, and sprinkle some salt.

Setting

Matching Mood
For some perfect less is more moments on a Sunday afternoon.

Matching Wine
Any funky Chardonnay from Burgundy or funky Chenin Blanc from the Loire Valley.

Matching Music
Electro and ambient from Belfast-based Phil Kieran is popular on Nobelhart's own playlist. Spice it up with some early Krautrock tunes to add the German touch.

Jordi Peris, Bar del Pla, Barcelona

Classics Reloaded

Our favourite tapas bar serves a classic of Catalan cuisine. Such dishes are Jordi's springboard to take them up to a new level

BARCELONA

Pig's Trotters

»This dish represents what we call Xup-Xup cuisine—it is slowly cooked. A Catalan stamp.«—Jordi Peris

Ingredients

Serves 2
2 pig's feet with skin in place for each person
6 peppercorns
½ garlic head, cut across
1 carrot, diced
½ leek, chopped into small pieces
Aromatic herbs: 1 teaspoon each of rosemary, basil, and thyme
1 onion, chopped
Almond paste (a clove of garlic chopped, one spoon of breadcrumbs, two almonds, one small spicy bicho pepper).
1 tomato, grated
A splash of stale wine

Preparation

1. Place the pig's feet in a pressure cooker and add all vegetables. Cook for 45 minutes. Let it cool. Take out the feet to make the terrine. Keep the broth to make the sofrito sauce later.

Terrine
1. Chop the meat and add salt, herbs.
2. Put meat on top of the skin and wrap the skin around to make two rolls. Place the underside of the skin in the bottom of a dish. Keep in the refrigerator for at least for two hours.

Almond paste
1. Finely chop all the ingredients and mix well. Set aside until needed.

Sofrito sauce
1. In a heavy-bottom frying pan add the broth along with its vegetables, chopped herbs, grated tomato, and wine. Over a medium heat stir often until it becomes a thick consistency.

Finish the dish
1. Cut the meat rolls in 4 pieces each.
2. Heat a skillet over a medium low heat and add the chopped meat from the pig's feet in the hot pan. Slow cooking is very important to warm the terrine, keeping it succulent and crispy on the top and bottom.
3. For serving, spoon the sofristo sauce onto the plate, then place four pieces of pork trotter. Finally sprinkle with the almond mix.

Setting

Matching Drink
A fresh natural red wine from the region—like the Mendall Espartal BP2 Anfora.

Matching Music
Jazz, flamenco, or rumba catalana.

Meeting Coney
Margot Guicheteau

The black and orange leather chairs contrasted against the blue and pale-yellow mosaic wall, a warm breeze goes from the door on Lafayette street, all along the corridor of the little restaurant to the other door on Michigan Avenue. It's still early at Lafayette Coney Island, Detroit. Ali and his team are getting ready for the intense lunch coming up

Just like every other day of the week. The only one that is talking is Romani, an immigrant from Eastern Europe, who comes from time to time to help the team—all Yemenites. He cuts the sausages and can't shut up about Romania. Ali is here to remind him that the United States has welcomed him with open arms. This is Detroit's legacy. Yemeni people working in a restaurant that was once owned by Greek immigrants, who live in Hamtramck, a neighbourhood that used to be inhabited solely by the Polish, and is now occupied by a slew of Middle Eastern communities. A different reality. The one where being American also means coming from somewhere else.

The pile of brownish pink sausages is finally ready. A few clients start to rush in. The routine begins. From one hand to the next, porous bread goes down the assembly line. The sausages in rows, cooked barley brown in a few minutes. As a sleight of hand passes, the sandwich is almost ready. Chili, molten plastic yellow mustard and onion squares cover everything. Done. The dog is dribbling. The plates are sliding down the counter. It's noon in Detroit. It's rush hour. At the counter, greasy fingers are grabbing chili dog after chili dog for $2.60. Only the fingers change. Thick ones, skinny ones, and tiny ones. They are the ones of the blue collar worker, the businessman from Bedrock, and the tourist from Germany. It seems as if they all made an appointment at Coney Island. The rhythm is going crescendo. The waiters are playing the showmen. One is proud of being able to hold seven plates at the same time. Laying them down on his two arms. The other one is showing a customer the fork trick. Where he stacks forks and toothpicks ten high.

The restaurant is getting empty already. They didn't even have time to finish broiling all the sausages, but the customers have already gone back to work. Whatever, it's now going to be calm until the night shift. Ali goes underground for a break, takes off his shoes and looks at a YouTube video of animals fighting. Later on he decides to go back up to chat with his coworkers about a video that he just found: the explanation of the Titanic sinking, in Arabic. The last two customers are debating.

"Lafayette is my Coney Island."
"I still stand for American next door"

A common discussion here. Because coneys are not just coneys.

"So let's go and have one from American"
"Let's do it"

The Lafayette fan swallows the last bite and is ready to, maybe, be converted. Concerned, he follows his friend—really excited.

Just next door, the interior is suddenly all about flash. Checkerboard mosaic for the floor and aluminium boards for the ceiling. The colour red dominates the scene.

"Did you know that this coney is the first one? Keros, a Greek immigrant came to Detroit and opened this restaurant, a few years later he brought his brother who opened the one we were just in."

Coney Island went through all the same storms the city did, yet remains the same. Between 1900 and 1919, 343,000 Greek and Macedonian people arrived, en masse, to the American continent. A lot passed through New York's Ellis Island and got inspired by the already existing Coney Island Dog. They imagined that doing a fast, cheap hot dog for the Motor City workers was going to be a profitable affair. And it was. They spread. Each with their own slightly different recipe.

"I heard that Duly's in South West is also a very iconic one, but for their breakfast."

Out the door again. They were starting a Coney Island competition.

This one is small and only has a counter. A blond woman, with a sweet smile, but a jaded eye, is taking the orders of the very excited duo. "Do you want to add grits?"

They did.

On the walls, three small black and white framed pictures are hanging above them, a big one with nine pictures of Anthony Bourdain, mouth wide open, round big eyes ready to swallow the dog. Next to it, the words he used to describe it: "It seems like a simple thing. Hot dog, chili, raw onions, mustard, steamed bun, but the delicate interplay between these ingredients when done right is symphonic." I thought it was just a hot dog. Not a classical orchestra.

A young boy is staring at it while eating one, almost mimicking the same face in the picture. The duo makes the connection and have a good laugh about it. They start interacting and all seem to get along pretty well. Twenty minutes later the boy jumps in his truck followed by the two coney island fans. After a short drive, they enter a big warehouse, on which is written Ross Coated Fabrics. In the back, a pile of yellow foam. A tall, robust man is cutting a coach with a dirty-green rusted machine.

"Tim, this guy from Hamtramck brought this oriental coach to cut up, I'll let you finish. Who are those two guys you are with?"

Very candidly, he answers, "Just two New Yorkers who came to eat the best coney around. And they still can't shut up about it."

That's what happens when you go from hot dog to hot dog. You end up in a fabric warehouse.

Margot Guicheteau is a French journalist who has written for French national newspaper "Le Figaro" and "Le Temps" in Switzerland. She moved several years ago to Detroit, exploring her Polish roots among the US's second largest community while documenting the city's unique and complex history.

Helga Haraldsdóttir, Matur og Drykkur, Reykjavik

Nostalgic Isle

A chef finds inspiration in Iceland's raw natural beauty

Reykjavik

Refining the Home Cooked

"Iceland is beautiful and has this almost fairy-tale look on the outside. But the nature here is very raw and you have to synchronise with it to use it to your advantage. Study the seasons, history, and produce, and you find this treasure chest of possibilities."

That is the bold statement of Helga Haraldsdóttir. Though her restaurant's name translates simply to "food and drink," it's anything but basic. The team researches old cookbooks and manuscripts to experiment with traditional Icelandic cuisine, producing creative reinterpretations. Much appreciated by diners tired of tourist-focussed classic dishes, the restaurant is dedicated to thoroughly making use of Iceland's natural bounty, from the creatures of the sea to the herbs lining the hills. As head chef, Helga is very aware of Iceland's culinary history and its natural landscape that make its dishes so unique. Here she shares a reinterpretation of a classic dish preferred by Iceland's fishermen who required serious fuel to sustain them in their work.

Salted Cod With Potato Purée, Confit Onion And Beurre Noisette

»Salted cod, potatoes, rye bread and lamb fat is a classic Icelandic dish. This recipe is a take on that on a bit more upscale level. When making this dish my goal was to make something nostalgic. I find food to be the most exciting when you find something familiar to it though it´s in a another costume.«—Helga Haraldsdóttir

Ingredients

Serves 2
500 g (1.1lbs) salted cod fillet, prepared—soak the salted cod in water for 2–3 days, change water 3 times a day. Cut into 2 pieces
400 g baking potatoes—about 2 large potatoes
200 ml (3/4 c) heavy cream
430 g (2 c plus 2 tbs) unsalted butter, divided
1 × small yellow onion (40–50 g), cut in half crosswise
Lamb fat, cut into small cubes—ask your local butcher
30 g (2 tbs) sunflower seeds
Zest of half a lemon
100 g (.22 lb) lamb fat
4–5 g green peppercorns or to taste, ground
Salt to taste
100g Icelandic sweet rye bread (dökkt rúgbrauð), cut into small cubes
—can be substituted with German rye bread or pumpernickel
Oil to fry

Preparation

Potato pureé
1. Preheat oven at 180°C/350°F
2. Bake potatoes for 50–60 minutes. Check doneness—the potatoes are cooked when you feel no resistance poking them with a wooden skewer or a knife
3. Cut hot potatoes in half and push through a sieve with a wooden spoon into a bowl. Discard the potato skin.
3. In a big pot over a medium heat add cream and 100g (½ cup) butter, bringing it to a boil.
4. Add the sieved potatoes to the cream and butter mixture and mix them to the consistency of your preference.
5. Season with salt—keep in mind that the cod is salted, so go lightly with it.

Beurre noisette and confit onion
1. In a saucepan over medium-low heat, melt 300 g (1½ cup) butter—keep about 30 g (2 tbs) of butter to make sweet rye bread crumbles. In the meantime, heat a skillet on another stove over a medium high heat until the skillet is very hot, add onion halves, cut side down without any fat or oil and grill them until they are dark brown. Take the grilled onion out and add to the pot with melted butter. Let it cook over medium-low heat for 20–30 minutes or until the onion is soft. Remove the cooked onion. Let them cool a bit and separate onion halves into single layers. Put them aside and keep warm until ready to serve.
2. Turn the heat up to a medium high. Let the butter cook until it becomes beurre noisette—when the fat and milk part are separated. The milk will continue cooking and turn solid and toasted. Remove the pot from the

heat. Once the milk starts to turn solid it will brown quickly. Keep an eye on this so it doesn't burn.

Lamb fat
1. Heat a saucepan over medium high and add a splash of oil.
Add the lamb fat to the hot saucepan, stir often so the fat doesn't stick and burn.
2. Once the fat becomes golden brown, lower the heat, and add sunflower seeds. Let it fry in the fat for a couple minutes.
3. Finish with lemon zest, pepper, and salt to taste. Put it aside until ready to serve.

Sweet rye bread crumble
1. Preheat oven to 160°C
2. Melt 30 g (2 tbs) butter
3. In a bowl big enough to toss the bread and butter together, toss them until the cubes are coated with melted butter.
4. Spread the bread cubes on a baking sheet and bake in the oven for 10 min to make croutons. Take the croutons out and let them cool completely.
5. In a mortar or food processor grind the croutons into crumble.

Salted cod
1. You need a pan which can go into the oven.
2. Preheat the oven to 180°C (350°F).
3. Heat a pan over medium-high heat, add the oil, and let it heat up until it starts to smoke lightly.
4. Pat dry the cod with a kitchen towel. if you want to keep the skin on, then fry on the skin side first. Fry both sides for 2–3 min or until golden brown, and add a bit of butter to the pan.
5. Finish the cod in the oven for 4–5 min or until it is flaky and easily falls apart.

Assembling the dish
In a warm deep dish, spoon the potato purée at the bottom then top with a cod fillet and generously spoon the beurre noisette over the fish. Add the sweet rye bread crumble on the side, add a few onion confit with a small dab of butter inside of each layer, and top with the lamb fat and roasted sunflower seeds.

Setting

Matching Mood
For a deep dive into Nordic cuisine on a long winter night.

Matching Drink
A crisp and aromatic Albariño from northwest Spain.

Matching Music
Minimalistic dub techno from Jón Brynjar Óskarsson and Moritz von Oswald's cooperation with the Norwegian Nils Petter Molvær.

Bruno Caseiro, Cavalariça, Comporta

Remix Atlantico

A Portuguese chef brings a classic fish dish to the next level

Tales from Alentejo

Comporta has gained popularity as a summer destination over the last ten years. Beautiful sandy beaches, the laidback lifestyle and fine fruits of land and sea make the former fishing village a flawless hideout for hot days.

These are also excellent conditions for a creative chef like Bruno Caseiro. In London he was trained at O Viajante, Nuno Mendes' Michelin-starred restaurant, and The Chiltern Firehouse. Since 2017, his wizardry has been employed in the kitchen of Cavalariça—a non-formal fine dining restaurant in a former horse stable south of Lisbon in Comporta. With his wife Filipa Gonçalves head of service, Bruno values a family vibe. The challenge for him is to apply an innovative perspective towards classic dishes—while remaining unpretentious and authentic. Fresh and local ingredients are the foundations of his edifice. That also goes for the recipe presented here: the sea bream comes from his neighbouring village of Carrasqueira, and is enhanced with an Asian twist.

Sea Bream Crudo With Citrus Sauce And Black Rice Crackers

»It brings together one of my favorite cuisines, Asian, with local fish and products like rice. It summarises how I like to eat and tell stories about what surrounds me through my food«
—Bruno Caseiro

Ingredients

Serves 2
1 × 400/500g (ca.90–1.10 lbs) sea bream, trimmed and scaled
100g (1 cup) miso paste
100g (1 cup) dashi
Dash of sesame oil to taste
Dash of fish sauce to taste
Juice and zest of 1 lime
100g Carolino rice (Portuguese rice)
600g (6 cups) water
5g (a generous 1 teaspoon) of squid ink from a jar
50g (1/2 cup) red onion, thinly sliced
50g (1/2 cup) physalis, cut in half
5g (a generous 1 teaspoon) pickled green jalapeños
5g dry kombu seaweed
Coriander leaves for garnish, chopped
100g (1 cup) rice vinegar
80g (1/2 Cup plus 2 ½ Tablespoons) sugar
Oil for frying rice crackers
Salt

Preparation

Fish
1. Fillet the sea bream and remove the skin.
2. Wrap the fillets in a cheesecloth. Spread the miso paste all around the cheesecloth. Put in glass shallow dish and cover with plastic wrap. Leave it to cure for 24 hours in refrigerator.

Rice cracker
1. In a pot over medium high heat, add 500g (5 cups) water and rice and bring it to boil. Lower the heat to medium and let it cook until it is completely overcooked and mushy. Let the rice cool down.
2. In a food processor add cooked rice, squid ink and blitz it. Make sure to leave it a bit grainy, not smooth.
3. Line a baking sheet with parchment paper and spread rice paste evenly. Let it completely dehydrate in the oven at 50°c (120°F), between 24 and 48 hours.
4. Break dry black rice paste with your hands into small pieces.
5. Heat oil in a deep-frying pan over medium heat, add the rice crackers in the hot oil and fry until it puffs. It can take a bit of time before the crackers start to puff. Once they puff, it goes quite quickly. Drain rice crackers on a rack or paper towels. Season with salt.

Dashi sauce
1. In a bowl combine dashi, sesame oil, fish sauce, lime juice and zest of lime. Taste to check seasoning.

Kombu Pickle

1. Make pickle brine in a saucepan, combine rice vinegar, sugar and 100g (1 cup) water and bring it to boil over medium heat.
In a heat proof bowl pure the hot pickle brine to dry kombu seaweed, red onion, and green jalapeños. Let the pickle cool down before serving.

Assemble the dish

Remove the fish from the miso cure. Cut into slices like sashimi.
Arrange the fish slices in a bowl, dress with the dashi and lime sauce, pickled kombu, red onion, pickled jalapeño slices and physalis.
Add the rice crackers and garnish with coriander leaves.

> Setting

Matching Mood

Even when the sea is far away, this feeds the desire for the smell of salt on your skin.

Matching Wine

2018 Pêgo da Moura Alfaiate. A fresh white from a local producer in the region, the grape varieties are Arinto, Antão Vaz and Sercial.

Matching Music

Bruno is a big fan of world music. He listens to Mayra Andrade's album "Manga" for cooking and recommends "In the Heart of the Moon" by Ali Farka Touré and Toumani Diabaté for eating.

Rice and fish, two staples of portuguese and japanese food, that come together to tell a story that goes back in time, to the travels, exchanges and relationships that influenced the east and the west we live in today.

Luis Rodriguez, Tabaré, New York City

Strictly Homemade

From Brooklyn to Uruguay's Italian heritage

Poem of Conquest

Even the name of this restaurant breathes with Uruguay's history. It refers to the epic poem of 1886 telling the tragic love story of Tabaré, from the Charrúa people, with the sister of a Spanish conquistador. The menu of course is also saturated with the vibe of the country, and the team of Bruno Gervais, Diego Pérez-Olave (pictured) and chef Luis Rodriguez, who rose from line cook to chef de cuisine, continues to experiment on the theme.

The country's strong European roots come through in all dishes; from the national staple of beef, or the pasta, a result of Italian immigration in the late 19th and early 20th centuries. With ths recipe for homemade pasta, Rodriguez expresses both Uruguay's Italian influence as well as a local tradition still developing today.

Potato & Beet Gnocchi, Mascarpone Cream & Crispy Sage

»Our homemade pasta is traditionally made on the 29th of each month, to follow the Uruguayan tradition.« —Luis Rodriguez

Ingredients

Serves 2
- 1 Idaho potato
- 1 Red beet
- 1 Egg yolk
- 300 g (3 cups) grated parmesan cheese
- 32 to 64 g (1/4 to 1/2 cup) of unbleached all-purpose flour
- 1 teaspoon salt
- ½ (1.7 g) teaspoon of black pepper
- Pinch of freshly grated nutmeg
- 1/2 cup (115 g) of Mascarpone cheese
- 14.18 g (2 tablespoons) of butter
- 15 g (2 tablespoons) of cornstarch
- 120 ml (1/2 cup) of dry white or rose wine
- A few sage leaves
- Olive oil

Preparation

1. Wrap the potato and beet each in their own sheet of aluminum foil. Place them in a 175°C (350°F) oven for 50–60 minutes (until soft). Remove the aluminum foil and let them stand just until cool enough to handle.
2. Scrape the skin and pass them through a ricer into a large bowl. Let cool until almost at room temperature, at least 20 minutes.
3. In a small bowl, beat the egg yolk, salt, pepper, and nutmeg together. In a large bowl, gather the cold potatoes and beets into a mound and form a well in the centre. Pour the egg mixture into the well and add parmesan cheese. Knead it together with both hands, gradually adding enough of the flour to form a smooth but slightly sticky dough. (Do not overmix, or the gnocchi will be tough).
4. Transfer it to a floured surface and wash your hands.
Cut the dough into two equal pieces. Place one piece in front of you and roll the dough into a rope 1/2-inch (1 cm) thick, flouring the dough if necessary as you roll to keep it from sticking.
5. With a sharp knife, cut the rope crosswise every ¾ inch (2 cm) to make roughly 3/4-inch-square gnocchi.
6. Arrange the gnocchi in a single layer on parchment-covered baking sheets, making sure they do not touch. Repeat until you run out of dough, re-flouring the work surface as needed. When all the gnocchi have been cut and spread out on the baking sheets, sprinkle them with a little more flour.
7. Bring a large pot of well-salted water to a boil. Drop the gnocchi into the boiling water.
8. Give one gentle stir, and wait until the gnocchi all float to the surface of the water.
9. Remove the gnocchi from the water with a slotted skimmer spoon, draining them well.

Sauce

1. Heat the olive oil in a skillet over medium-high heat until hot. Fry the sage leaves for a couple of seconds until crisp, take them out and place them on a paper towel.
2. Into the same skillet add cornstarch, stirring constantly with a whisk until blended. Add the mascarpone cheese. Stir slowly while you add the wine, add salt, and freshly ground pepper to taste.

Assembling the dish

Divide the sauce between the two plates, place carefully the gnocchi on top of the sauce and finish with the sage leaves, grated parmesan cheese, and a drizzle of extra virgin olive oil.

Setting

Matching Mood
The perfect ground to prepare for a long weekend night.

Matching Drink
Uruguay produces excellent merlot—try an Antigua Bodega Stagnari Osiris.

Matching Music
A colourful mix of vibrant tracks from Italy featuring Donatella Viggiano, Lucio Battisti and Erlend Øye.

Jonathan Woolway, St. John, London

Nose-to-Tail Perfection

One of London's favourite chefs shares his signature supper for two

Good Food is Timeless

A lot of people may call St. John in London an institution, but this grand compliment has definitely not inflated the egos of the staff, who like to keep things humble and just consistently delicious. A restaurant appropriate for any time of day or night, any and all seasons, St. John is like a reliable friend who feeds you classic British fare done well, cocktails mixed just right, and even a simple comforting pint. It's not quite a typical British restaurant though, since its menu plays with French and Italian cooking traditions, always bringing something new to the table. Chef Jonathan Woolway also happens to be passionate about the nose-to-tail philosophy, which has over time become synonymous with the restaurant's ethos. No parts are ever wasted, which rings especially true for the recipe of half a pig's head included here.

Jonathan, St. John is often thought of as a London food institution. What are the challenges of such a title and how can you remain relevant and exciting?

"Institution" is a word that has been bestowed on us from the outside. Within our bubble, we confidently and humbly continue to do as we have always done. We have never really been in fashion. When St. John first opened, we were accused of being 200 years out of date—which was a great compliment! Trends and fads are usually a tragedy in food; good food is timeless. Our recipes are in a constant state of evolution—they are not refined, but an evolving, subliminal comment on our nature. As our founder Fergus Henderson says, "We are always and yet never the same."

You have a "nose to tail," approach when it comes to your menu. Where do you get your ingredients to ensure your high standard?

We work with excellent suppliers, most of whom have been with us since day one. Richard Vaughan of Huntsham Farm supplies us with the rare breed of Middle White pigs (used in this dish). They take their role in the farm-to-table process extremely seriously, which makes our life easy. It's a joy to work with them. Similarly, each morning we call our fish suppliers and ask them, "What's good? What's available?" Our nose-to-tail philosophy is about holistic eating. We are led by our suppliers and the seasons. It's common sense to make use of the delights, afforded by nature, at the place and very moment of their prime.

If people wanted a bit of St. John at home, what are some essentials you'd recommend?

A well-stocked store is a magician's briefcase, containing everything you need to conjure something out of nothing, like lentils or a jar of Opies pickled walnuts. We also say a brine bucket is your best friend. Think of it as Heathrow Terminal 5, from which each delicious part can be taken when the time is right, each to its exciting destination. Then there are dressings, the engine oil and lubrication of our menus. Our Green Sauce, ubiquitous and marvellous in equal measure ... or perhaps a jar of mayonnaise—have the power to transform the mundane into something spectacular! And finally, don't forget bread and butter, and perhaps a bottle of something lovely up your sleeve.

Pot Roast Half Pig's Head

»Our dish is a perfect romantic supper for two. Imagine gazing into the eyes of your loved one over a golden pig's cheek, ear or snout!«—Jonathan Woolway

Ingredients

Serves 2
A dollop of duck fat
8 shallots, peeled and left whole
8 cloves of garlic, peeled and left whole
½ pig's head (we use Middle White, a rare breed, as half its head is perfectly sized for two people)
1 glass of Calvados
A bundle of joy (tie together parsley stalks, thyme, rosemary, bay, and sage)
½ bottle of white wine
Chicken stock
Sea salt and black pepper
A healthy spoonful of Dijon mustard
A bunch of watercress, trimmed

Preparation

1. Preheat oven (180°C/350°F)
2. In a stainless steel roasting pan (wide and deep enough to accommodate half a pig's head) add a dollop of the duck fat. Melt the fat in the roasting pan over medium heat on the stove, add shallots and garlic, and leave them

to do a little sweating to improve the flavour of the dish. Shuggle the roasting pan occasionally to prevent any burning, but you do want some colour.
3. When happy with these, cover the ear of your demi-head with foil so it doesn't frazzle, and put the pig head in the roasting pan. Pour a glass of Calvados over the head to welcome it to its new environment, add the wine and then the chicken stock.
4. What you are looking for, is the pig's head to lurk in the stock like an alligator in a swamp.
5. Season with salt and pepper, cover the roasting pan with greaseproof paper and place in the oven for 3 hours, until the head is totally giving. Check it after 2–2½ hours—you could remove the greaseproof paper at this point and get a little colour on the cheek.
6. When ready, remove the head to a warm plate. Whisk the Dijon mustard into the roasting pan with hot liquid then add a bunch of watercress to wilt.

Assembling the dish
Serve family style on a large warm platter—perfect for sharing. Make a pillow of shallots and garlic and wilted watercress, upon which you can rest the pig's head.

Side dish suggestions
Buttered Jersey Royal potatoes (if the time of year is right) and perhaps a cleansing cucumber, butterhead, and lovage salad.

Matching mood
Romantic dinners for non faint-at-heart couples.

Matching Drink
A fresh Riesling from the next generation of winemakers—try the 2018 Zugpferd "i.d.R." Sausenheimer Hütt Riesling trocken from Karoline & Dorothee Gaul.

Matching Music
Jazz from legends like Miles Davis or John Coltrane, spiced up with some ska from the island.

Living Food
What a British Food Critic Doesn't Know About Korean Food
Jieun Choi

Arguably the most reputable restaurant guide in the world, the Michelin Guide is a matter of life and death for some seasoned chefs. Earning a star not only drives hundreds of eager gourmets to the restaurant, but also vests the chef with a sense of accomplishment. The debut of the Michelin Guide in Seoul last November, therefore, signaled that the South Korean gastronomy scene was on a par with countries that have longer pedigrees of fine dining, like France and Italy

A total of 24 restaurants in Seoul were given at least a star, 13 of them serving Korean cuisine. Two Korean restaurants were given the highest denomination of three Michelin stars: *Gaon* and *La Yeon*. Many South Koreans, known for their obsession with promoting Korean cuisine overseas, welcomed the stars enthusiastically. But some critics had misgivings about Michelin's generosity.

One of them was British food critic Andy Hayler, who claims to have eaten in all the Michelin three-star restaurants in the world since 2004, including in *Gaon* and *La Yeon*. Much to Hayler's consternation, his visits to the restaurants, which should provide "exceptional cuisine that is worth a special journey" (Michelin's definition of three-starred restaurants), were less than satisfying.

According to Hayler, despite the good ambience and excellent service, the food itself did not stand out compared to the Korean food he ate elsewhere — mostly places with big Korean migrant communities, like Los Angeles, Tokyo and New Malden in London. In an interview with *Korea Exposé*, he admitted that he is no Korean food expert, but asserted that this does not disqualify him from distinguishing the remarkable from the good.

He pointed out the ingredients that fell short of the high standards that Michelin usually holds. Standard ingredients like beef, chicken and seafood were "fine" but not exceptional. To Hayler, what Korean cuisine really lacks—in general, not just at *Gaon* and *La Yeon*—are luxury ingredients like white truffle. "Can you compare kimchi to risotto with white truffles? Certainly not," he said. "There are some limits to what you can really do with some pickled garlic or pickled cabbage."

Hur Jae-in, co-founder of *GBB Kitchen*, a Seoul-based cooking studio, and a gourmet who has dined in at least 150 Michelin-starred restaurants worldwide, said Hayler's assessment of Korean cuisine is narrow-minded.

"Of course you can't compare white truffle risotto with kimchi. Truffle is a delicacy that goes well with any dish. Of course people would instinctively feel that [the truffle's] umami flavour is more appetizing than the sour kimchi," she said. "There are so many different types of kimchi. The flavours change depending on who is making the kimchi, and how much the person uses the different spices, the salts, the type of salted seafood, etc."

Hur said that a "perfect mathematical formula" exists for a white truffle risotto, which not many chefs have the technical expertise to master, whereas there is no textbook answer for kimchi, the taste of which is more a matter of preference. Even South Koreans can't identify the "perfect kimchi." It's possible—and likely—for people to prefer kimchi from a small bibimbap place in a village nowhere, than the ones served at Gaon and La Yeon.

But another Korean food expert, who asked to be identified only by his surname Park, said that South Korea does lack fine and rare ingredients because ingredient varieties are limited by the country's small and relatively homogenous landscape. The overall dry climate, save torrential downpours in the summer, stymies abundant growth of flora and fauna. Many ingredients in Korean cuisine originated from abroad, including a main ingredient for kimchi, red pepper, which originates from Latin America and is thought to have been introduced to Korea through Japan in the late 16th century.

Like Michelin inspectors, British food critic Hayler might have been similarly misinformed about Korean cuisine. Invoking his experience with French cuisine, Hayler bemoaned the level of technical prowess at Gaon and La Yeon, and by extension doubted the technical capabilities of Korean cuisine in general. He found Korean desserts rather simple, compared to French pastry, which calls for hours of preparation and years of mastery. He also equated the absence of an "elaborate French sauce like demi-glace" to an absence of technical skill.

But this, for Hur, shows Hayler's lack of understanding. "Making traditional Korean sauce, like soy bean paste and red pepper paste, takes a lot longer and requires professional skill," she said, adding that the purpose of fermentation was not only for the taste, but also for preservation, which is not the case for demi-glace.
But Park and Hur think the inspectors still lacked proper understanding of traditional Korean cuisine, which is innately different from French and Japanese cuisines. What the inspectors overlooked is that traditional Korean cuisine serves a number of dishes at once. "Traditional Korean food is not a 'dish.' Instead, sundry side dishes with rice and soup are served altogether on the table. The 'dish' is created inside one's mouth, by combining the different foods. So each person has a different experience even when he or she shares the same table with others," said Park.

And traditional Korean cuisine is not served à la carte, which means it is difficult to recreate a fine dining experience, almost

always served as table d'hôte—a multi-course meal—in the West. Hur said she had not been to either of the three-starred restaurants in Seoul, precisely because of her unfamiliarity with and bias against traditional Korean meals rendered in a course format. "Even kings did not eat a course meal in Korea," said Hur. Over the years, the Michelin Guide has been criticized for being biased towards French and Japanese cuisines. Last year, Japan had the most number of three-Michelin-starred restaurants, 32 to be exact, and France had 26. While the Guide withholds its exact assessment criteria, it highlights the importance of ingredient quality, techniques, originality, value for money and consistency in execution.

Since 2009, the South Korean government has spent millions of dollars introducing Korean food to the global audience. The efforts of the "K-Food globalization project" included creating a top-tier Korean restaurant in Manhattan (which was never realized), publishing cookbooks in multiple languages and setting a taskforce to with K-Food on UNESCO's intangible cultural heritage list. Over the past eight years, Korea's Ministry of Agriculture, Food and Rural Affairs spent 153 billion won (135 million dollars) on the project alone.

Michelin's ad revenue from the Korean government doesn't necessarily mean the Guide was biased more favorably toward Korean restaurants. The Seoul Guide has certainly helped the government's K-food promotion, but it has also had unintended consequences. Gaon and La Yeon's three stars are fuelling debate about whether they deserve the acclaim, whether Korean food meets the Michelin criteria, and whether Michelin understands Korean cuisine.

Hur Jae-in is not too concerned. "The inaugural Michelin Guide need not be the correct answer," she said. "Even in New York City, where competition is more fierce, the number of Michelin stars changes every year. Think about how many of South Korea's stars would change in the future."

Jieun Choi is a photographer and journalist who covers politics, society, the art world and food. She has worked in Seoul and Melbourne.

Lee Christopher Thompson, St. Bart, Berlin

Cross Border

An Aussie chef presents a Russian dessert in a British-style gastropub

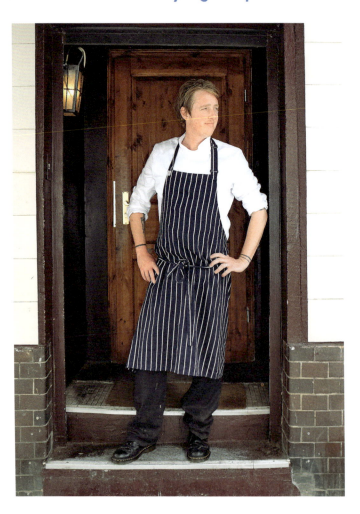

Inspiration out of Necessity

Australian-born Lee Christopher Thompson is not a trained chef, but what he lacks in accolades, he makes up for with a menu of honest and delicious food that's taken a stronghold in Berlin's Kreuzberg district. St. Bart is not a British pub and it definitely doesn't serve your usual ale-appropriate grub. Instead, Lee and his team create dishes on a whim, meant to be shared and to go rather well with rounds of wine or cocktails or beer. From a bacon sandwich or smoked mackerel with raw and pickled rhubarb and watercress, the St. Bart creations are never boring.

Here Lee is sharing something sweet, a pavlova bound to please any dessert lover. It can either be baked in a normal oven in one giant delicious lump or made into smaller portions for a more aesthetic effect.

Lee, what's the story behind the Pavlova?

It's my mum's recipe. It's also got a complicated culinary history, from the Spanische Windtorte in 17th-century Germany to a Russian ballerina in Australia in the 1920s, or possibly New Zealand. Apart from that it can be made the day before and will make people happy.

St. Bart's cuisine is difficult to classify and has been called "German-Antipodean." What's the real inspiration behind your dishes?

I think our dishes reflect what we are: a weird Aussie-German mix with a tendency to overdo it when it comes to fat and acid. It's the season that dictates what we serve. If it's good and we want to eat it ourselves, then it lands on the menu; inspiration out of necessity.

Why did you decide to open a restaurant in Berlin and how does the city affect your cooking?

The real story is I met a girl named Nadin when I was a dishwasher and decided to make Berlin my home. I had the privilege to learn a language and a trade, while experiencing the true nature of the city with a local lady. From day one the name "public house" has been our mantra at St. Bart. Our highest aspiration is to be a solid neighbourhood place so the already endemic seasonal traditions in this city affect us on a daily basis.

Rosewater Pavlova

The meringue-based dessert was named after Russian ballerina Anna Pavlova in the 1920s.

Ingredients

Serves 2–3

Bramble rosewater compote
500 g (3 ½ cups) blackberries
250 g (1 cup) brown sugar
7 sprigs of thyme
500 ml (2 cups + 2 tbsp) water
50 ml (1/4 cup) rosewater

Pavlova
210 g egg whites (about 6 medium eggs)
240 g (2 heaped cups) powdered sugar
15 ml (1 tbsp) white wine vinegar
200 ml (almost 1 cup) whipping cream
200 g (1 1/5 cup) fresh blackberries for decoration

Preparation

Bramble rosewater compote
1. Combine all the ingredients for the bramble compote in a small saucepan. Cook on a low heat for about an hour or until everything has turned into a sticky sauce or a watery jam. Set aside.

Pavlova
1. In an electric mixing bowl, whip the egg white on a low speed until soft, about 7 minutes. Add all the powdered sugar at once and mix on a higher speed until the mixture becomes glossy and stiff, about 7 minutes. Add the white wine vinegar, and whip to combine.
2. Preheat your oven at 110°C (230°F). Line a baking sheet with baking paper, then spoon or use a pastry bag in a circular motion to form the meringue. You can divide it into six smaller individual pavlovas or make one big pavlova as you wish. Bake for about 1h50m. Remove from the oven and allow to cool. Whip the cream in an electric mixing bowl.

Assembling the dish
Heap the whipped cream on top of the pavlova until the weight makes it collapse. Spoon the compote onto the cream, and garnish with blackberries and powdered sugar.

Setting

Matching Mood
To be shared by lovers who've had it all before.

Matching Drink
Russian Caravan tea.

Matching Music
Classical music from early 20th-century Russian composers like Shostakovich, Stravinsky, or Prokofiev.

Ingredients

Ingredient lists are available on your smartphone via the following QR codes. Simply scan the codes with your camera app

Playlists

Playlists are available for all recipes. Scan the QR codes below and access them on Spotify

Crab Rangoons
→ p. 7

Tabbouleh
→ p. 11

Salmon Ceviche
→ p. 15

Kejriwal
→ p. 18–19

Celeriac and Blackcurrant Wood Oil
→ p. 22–23

Pig's Trotters
→ p. 25

Salted Cod
→ p. 32–33

Sea Bream Crudo
→ p. 36–37

Potato & Beet Gnocchi
→ p. 42–43

Pot Roast Half Pig's Head
→ p. 47, 48

Rosewater Pavlova
→ p. 58–59

re too short meals.

Make sure they're all good with the LOST iN app.

Download on the App Store
GET IT ON Google Play

Available from LOST iN

…and Austin, Dusseldorf, Edinburgh, Hamburg, Helsinki, Marseille, Oslo, Porto, Reykjavik, Rotterdam, Seattle, Sydney, Tangier, Tel Aviv, Toronto in the LOST iN Mobile App.

LOSTIN.COM